Because No One Told Me: 21 Days of Purposeful Transfiguration for Adolescents

Dedicated to....

God for keeping me, My Husband for loving me, My Children for needing me, my Family for supporting me, and the Youth for inspiring me.

Table of Contents:

Preface

Day 1- Your Purpose Exceeds Your Pain

Day 2- Well Done!

Day 3- Your Talents vs. Your Spiritual Gifts

Day 4- But, I want to be loved

Day 5- Why You Matter

Day 6- Center Yourself through Meditation

Day 7- You Deserve God's Grace

Day 8- Divine Design

Day 9- Be here, Living in the Present Tense, Right Now!

Day 10- Fear

Day 11- Mistakes=Excellence

Day 12- Never Be Tasteless

Day 13- Your Pace, Your Race

Day 14- Who are Your Friends?

Day 15- Healthy Decisions

Day 16- Who Inspires You?

Day 17- Broken Crayons Still Color & Dirty Hands Still Pray!

Day 18- Stop Making Excuses

Day 19- Your Haters are required to Witness Your Glow Up!

Day 20- SMART Goals

Day 21- Lean on me – The Importance of Mentorship

Preface

In my life there have been many times that I was looking for a new beginning, especially after having suffered something tragic, having made horrible mistakes, or having been left heartbroken. I chose 21 days for this Journal because of the meaning that stands behind 21.Biblically, the number 21 has both positive and negative meanings. Negatively speaking, 21 helps define sin, mistakes, and rebellion; however, 21 also means "new beginnings" and the commencement of the next cycle in life, which in turn means that past life has ended so that one can start new. My professional and personal life has lead me to have a passion for helping young people like me who just need someone to help them along the way and tell them the things that they wish they'd known when they were younger.

My childhood was great! I mean from the outside looking in you would see no flaws. However, many times things are not always what they seem. Two loving parents, a great Godmother, the latest clothes, cell phones, and plenty of support from family. However, I was missing something. I did not understand my purpose. It did not matter how much my family affirmed me positively, I was lost. It was the people on the outside and the situations I got myself into that caused me to hit many roadblocks in finding God's purpose for my life.

This Journal will help you understand who you are in the Kingdom as God has planned for you. Upon finishing these readings and journaling you will understand what to do in certain situations and how to respond accordingly when the enemy tries to block your pathways. Although I cannot assure that you may not see some bumps in the road, I can help! I will tell you everything that I now know about purpose and navigating one of the hardest times in your life, adolescence.

You will begin to form into a more spiritual being as your transfiguration process becomes a purposeful journey. Please take this process seriously over the next 21 days as I walk you through understanding your purpose and tell you everything I wish someone would have told me.

Day 1: Your Purpose Exceeds Your Pain!

You are young, and it is possible that many things you have seen or been through thus far have been unfair. You went through what you did for a reason! Whether you realize it now or later, someone including you will be able to grow from that experience that God had you to go through specifically. We also know that God has never placed us in situations that we are not equipped to handle. The difference between you overcoming your pain is nothing short of recognizing the tricks of the enemy exactly as they are and looking to God for guidance.

Pain is often a part of the journey on the road of faith and spiritual maturity. Whatever God is urging you to clear away cannot be compared to what He ultimately wants to bring you. Only you can decide how your fires will affect you. Will you be sanctified or scarred? Are you going to allow God to prune you? Will you allow him to trim away the unwanted distractions that are robbing your purposeful fruit vines of nourishment?

When I was younger I suffered many painful experiences both physically and mentally. Although some of those experiences had seemed to be greater than the next, they all had one common denominator: my reaction. I would react in a negative way towards negative experiences and feelings, not knowing that if I had overpowered those negative feelings with positive ones the outcome would be not only beneficial to me, but those around me as well. I was reacting to the situations and not responding accordingly. I allowed my pain to exceed my purpose, which was so backwards. I did not think that I was good enough or beyond responding negatively to all that life brought to me in fear of what others thought. I wanted to be cool and, at that time, being cool did not mean being positive and allowing the Holy Spirit in my life to help me make the right decisions every day. There was much that had to be learned; the first step to not enduring so much pain was changing my reaction. The second was clearing away the negative people, places, and things that God told me not to associate myself with.

So today I say, 'Hey 12-year-old Jasmine! You have to tear down that stronghold of thinking you aren't better than what life throws at you! This faulty thinking pattern based on lies and deception is not what God wants for you! 2 Corinthians 10:4-5, "(for the weapons of our warfare are not of the flesh, but mighty before God to the casting down of strongholds); casting down imaginations, and every high thing that is exalted against the knowledge of God and bringing every thought into captivity to the obedience of Christ" You must see yourself and be in a different light and frame of mind!

Today in Your Journal: *Think of a negative situation that you were in recently, how did you react? How could you have responded differently?*

Day 2: Well done!

Knowing the purpose that God has planned for your life is very important! It is also important to know when your aspirations and desires are true to who you believe you are. Are they coming from a place of competition with others, or have you sought God to see what He in fact wants you to do? Are you seeking to please yourself or are you looking to please God in all that you do? It is imperative that you know the difference and fast because knowing could save you a lifetime of pain and unwanted detours to your destiny.

As a young girl I was very ambitious, but that ambition came from the accolades of being noticed as the "smart one" or the one who "wasn't like the other girls." I wasn't knowledgeable on how ambition and your true aspirations started with seeking God first wanting to ultimately please him. I found myself only wanting to achieve certain things because I knew that others would be proud of me or notice me. I had no clue that at the end of the day, I should work to please God through all of my endeavors. I also found that some of my aspirations were altered because I'd often want to live out other people's dreams because it sounded cool. But, I had to understand that my aspirations and desires were meant to be individualized because God only created one me; and I had to seek counsel from Him on what to do with He has given me.

So, to the younger me I say, 'Jasmine when you are seeking approval from others remember Galatians 1:10 (NIV) "Am I now trying to win the approval of human beings, or of God? Or am I trying to please people? If I were still trying to please people, I would not be a servant of Christ." Young Self, you are a true servant of Christ and you are to only serve Him; you do not need approval or accolades from others. Each day that you are working in your purpose you must make sure that it's in excellence because the greatest acknowledgment you can have is this: when you meet your heavenly Father again and He says, "Well done."

Today in your Journal: *Are the things that you do in life meant to please God? If not, how can you change that?*

Day 3: Your Talents vs. Your Spiritual Gifts

You can sing girl! You are wise! Although these may both seem like great "compliments" they are both so very different. When I was younger I had no clue what the difference was between a talent and a spiritual gift; and, although they both come from the same source they cannot compare. The first thing is that talents (Ephesians 2:10) are inherited and spiritual gifts (1 Peter 4:10-11, 1 Corinthians 12:7-11) are received, meaning that a gift is a natural ability that can be worked within your flesh for the greater good. Although your natural gifts are embedded in you genetically when you are born; your spiritual gifts come directly from the Spirit of God when you are born again and accept Jesus as your Savior.

I find that it is very important to understand your spiritual gifts during adolescence because this will truly become the beginning of walking in your purpose. Although your talents are developed and somewhat expected, your gifts are increased as you mature in your relationship with God. And, this does not mean the more you go to church, but the more you spend time with God talking, praying, and studying His word. When you are young it is so important to develop a strong relationship with Him, because trust me it will save you many unnecessary roadblocks to your destiny and adulthood.

God will continue to gift you beyond your natural talent so it so very important that we are open to hearing the many assignments that He will be giving us. God will give you the strength that you need to be great at what you do and to excel in your purpose, natural talents, and spiritual gifts. Daniel 11:32 says that "those who know their God shall be strong and will do great!" So, there is nothing that you cannot do with God and a strong relationship with Him.

    Lastly, remember to always use both your talents and spiritual gifts to serve God. Oftentimes, we use our talents for our own selfish reasons and self-gratification; and, there couldn't be a faster road to self-destruction. If it wasn't for God, we would not have these talents. You would not be able to open your mouth to sing, hear a tune, or even use your limbs to catch a football. Growing up I would often hear some of my peers say, "God didn't do this for me, I worked for this", but who woke you up, so you can work? If it weren't for God nothing you say, do, or imagine would be possible. Spiritual gifts are given to us, so we can give back to God as we serve His purpose of guiding other non-believers to His love. Every person is gifted in one or many ways. Although some may be strong or more matured than others, start operating in your gift! You can't just sit back and allow your pastor to do "all" the work. The Body of Christ needs you for a specific reason because your impact and purpose is unique, and the sooner you start operating in those gifts the faster the Kingdom expands.

    Young woman of God you are talented, however it is more profound and liberating to understand that the spiritual gifts God has given you can build the Family of God. Take a spiritual gifts tests, find out what they are, and lean on God's promises for your life so that you can begin to operate in His purpose for your life. As your relationship with God matures you will see your spiritual gifts blossom. Remember that, just because you're talented in a certain area, doesn't mean that talent is how God wants to manifest His purpose in you. Never be stagnant because it will result in an unfulfilled life.

Today in your Journal: *Do you know what your spiritual gifts are? If not, take a spirituals gifts test. You may find many online. Then answer, how do you think they fit in your life?*

Day 4: But, I want to be loved.

I will never forget when I had my first crush on a boy. And, I wanted him to know so badly that I went out of my way to see him, talk to him, and look nice in his presence. Long story short, he never even noticed me! I was heartbroken when I found out that he and my friend where "going together." When I look back on that part of my life and other times that were similar, I was so foolish! Why am I going out of my way for a person to know me when they ultimately can do nothing for me? It was very selfish of me because here I am with God Who sees me everywhere I go because He is omnipresent (Job 34:21), who hears me because He is always listening (1 John 5:15), and I am perfect in His sight (Hebrews 10:14); and yet, I still yearned the love of this boy, even though God loves me unconditionally. When we are young it is very imperative to understand that God loves us, and we should strive to love Him back as life progresses.

Later in life I learned that my adolescent years (10-19) was the wrong time to be focusing on the opposite sex because God had greater things for me ahead! If we learn our purpose or begin to seek God for our purpose at a young age, it will save us from so many heartaches from men in the future. That little boy broke my heart as did many other boys. But had I known that God will never leave me nor forsake me (Deuteronomy 31:6) I would have yearned for His love more than that boy. Adolescence is not a time to date, it's a time for development to find God in yourself so that you won't be tricked in the end. Unfortunately, I got this too late because I became an unwed mother at 19, but that doesn't have to be you!

Younger me, God loves you more than you will ever understand! You may have family and friends that break your heart; but, trust me when I say God will always love you unconditionally. In man's eyes we do not deserve the love He gives us, but to Him we deserve the ultimate sacrifice! He loves you so much that He used our Redeemer who lived a perfect life as a sacrifice so that we can have eternal life! (John 3:16) Now, if that isn't love I don't know what that is. Jesus died for you, and God gave you dominion over this world. So tell me, what do you want a chocolate rose from that little boy on Valentine's Day that cost $2, or the dominion and power that God has given you to rule this earth which is priceless?

Today in your Journal: *Have you ever had your heart broken by someone? If so, how did you handle it? Knowing what you know now, how will that change your future when it comes to love?*

Day 5: Why You matter

      When I was younger there were points in my life that I felt as if I did not matter and did not have a voice. Where I was from in Atlantic City if you aren't into what everyone else is doing you might as well be invisible. I had to learn that it wasn't that I didn't matter; it was just that I was different and no one in my neighborhood was willing to accept that. I learned to not look for their acceptance, but rather the acceptance of God. God sent me a true blessing to mold me at a young age. She was the reason many of my bad decisions turned out to be not so bad, because I had someone there to see me through.

      My spiritual mother was not your typical church mother, but she sure did know her word. She kept me as well as the other "vessels" in check, allowing us to make mistakes, but keeping us close enough that she can console us when we needed her the most. This woman had three daughters of her own, and I could never understand why she invested so much in young ladies like myself. She gave us unconditional love and the most important lesson she could ever teach us. Other than her many talks about STD'S and why boys are dirty, her most important lesson was that we matter. She always taught us that, no matter what, there is always someone that is looking at us and will be inspired by our walk with God and the purpose that we have for our life.

      Oftentimes, Mrs. J would clothe me in purple or have me minister with a purple scarf while praise dancing; she'd tell me that I was royalty, and I had power, dignity, and plenty wisdom. Purple represents a Proverbs 31 Woman. Proverbs 31:22 talks about the virtuous woman stating that, "she makes tapestry for herself; her clothing is of fine linen and purple." I find myself looking back on those days and realizing now more than ever that she saw something in me that I did not. She would tell me specifically that I had a calling on my life to teach the word of God and counsel others because I had a Steward's Heart (1 Peter 4:10). She knew that I would use my gift to serve God and his people, but I did not want to acknowledge it. I ran from that gift for as long as I could until I got older and actually made a profession of it as a social worker.

Subsequently, I then ran from my gift of teaching and preaching until I would always find myself speaking to groups of people about God and how He has truly changed my life. Sometimes I wonder how much stronger my relationship with God would be if I would have listened to her sooner than later. And if the revelation of everything she had said to me hadn't come until her untimely death. If I could go back in time I would definitely tell my younger self not to run from God because you want to fit in with what others are doing. Younger Jasmine, you matter, so listen to those meaningful figures around you that tell you so.

Today in your Journal: *What sets you apart from other people?*

Day 6: Center Yourself through Meditation

Meditation can most easily be described as training the mind. I started going to the gym and doing my version of "weight training" in high school, so I definitely know what it is to train; however, your "mind training" takes a whole lot of time and dedication. Growing up, there was always someone that, when they wanted to hurt you, they'd attack your mind rather than your physical body. The enemy works through these people to build wedges between you, God, and your purpose as much as he can. That is why centering yourself and mediation is just as important as prayer.

Mental health and mediation are two things that you just weren't hearing too much about back when I was going to church as a young girl, however it was so needed. There were many girls just like me that used church as an escape from their violent neighborhoods and homes. But, Sunday School and the preacher, telling us to pray and shout, did nothing for the mental strain we were experiencing. Learning to meditate can be difficult at first, from finding a quiet space to actually having the patience to give it time to work. Meditating, centering yourself, and becoming mindful of what is going on within you can be the beginning to a very peaceful life (Psalm 104:34).

I find that now more than ever young people like yourself are going through things that years ago were not heard of. The impact of certain avenues such as social media (and how easily it can be used in a negative manner) opens the doors for you and your peers to go through horrible situations. I identify with that, growing up I was bullied and suffered from depression in silence, but had I known about meditating and other holistic approaches things would have been so much easier. So today, take the advice I would give a young me suffering in silence: research mediation, find a quiet place, and begin to center yourself through meditation.

Today in your Journal: *Are there certain areas in your life that you would like to meditate on? And, why?*

Day 7: You Deserve God's Grace

Growing up *grace* to me meant the time that you were given to be a few minutes late to class without a penalty or having to get a late pass, but the Bible has a totally different meaning with kind of the same concept. Grace is defined as unmerited and undeserved favor from God (Ephesians 2:8-9) which means that no matter what you do God will continually give you the gift of Grace. God is perfect! Grace is His way of helping us have a relationship with Him despite the fact that we are imperfect in many ways.

While you are on your way to discovering your purpose and developing your relationship with God, you will make mistakes and plenty of them! I grew up in church, but that did not stop me from sneaking out the house, going to see boys, and drinking when I had no business doing so. Still, do you think God said," I taught you better than that, you are cut off!" Absolutely not! This did nothing but have me come to realization that, no matter what I do, the Holy Spirit was right there with me as I did these horrible things convicting me in every way possible.

I will never forget one weekend, after going to a youth service of singing and shouting, a couple of girls from church and I went to the movies. The movies on a Friday night was always packed, especially in the summer time. When we got there, we noticed a group of boys that kept looking at us. I really didn't pay them any mind until one of them walked up talking about his expensive car that he had outside. My friends and I went outside to see because the movie didn't start for about twenty minutes. Once we got to the car, he asked me if I wanted to take a ride and I said yes. I was only in the car for about 5 minutes, but it seemed like the longest ride of my life!

In the car he tried to kiss me and go up my skirt, no matter how many times I said no, he kept going. Finally, he got annoyed and took me back to the theater. I told no one what happened as he basically threw me out of his car. I went home as if nothing happened and told my parents nothing to this day. The next week I found out that boy had tried that with a couple of other girls that I knew. I was devastated and cried out to God because I didn't know what I did to deserve to be saved from being raped and possibly contracting a disease. That was nothing but His Grace!

After a youth service full of learning about how you should please God and how to take care of your temple as young woman I still managed to end up in what could have been a tragic situation. But by His grace I was saved and able to get away. Although I have many emotional scars from that incident, God has continuously given me grace even when I didn't want to align myself with the Holy Spirit. Younger me, don't beat yourself up because you know you knew better; but do not do it again! Tell someone you trust about what happened, and remember God will always take care of you no matter what situation you end up in because He has given you grace. You may not feel as if you deserve it, but you do because He is your father and will always protect you.

Today in your Journal: *Have you ever been in a situation where God's Grace seems undeserved? What did you change after that incident?*

Day 8: Divine Design

Now that you have learned about grace, it is very important to learn about what comes in the scripture directly after that. Ephesians 2:8-10 says, "For by grace you have been saved through faith. And this is not your own doing; it is the gift of God, not a result of works, so that no one may boast. For we are his workmanship, created in Christ Jesus for good works, which God prepared beforehand, that we should walk in them." This means that on your path to discovering your purpose you must understand that you are a divine design, a true workmanship created by God. You are unique in many ways and you should appreciate that in more ways than one.

As my life progressed, I learned that a good place to begin my search for God's purpose for my life was to understand that it was woven into every cell, tissue, and hair strand on my body. Oftentimes I would compare myself to others, especially the girls who seemed to have "more" than me. I would look around in middle school and see girls who were already developed, had larger breasts than my mother's, and butts that could dub as basketballs. I really did not understand why God made me awkwardly tall, underdeveloped, with big feet, and skinny as a toothpick. To this day I still look back on pictures and see a girl who did not know who she was and who could not look past her physical appearance because it was so much different than everyone else's. As a result, I became very insecure, and this is what I do not want for you.

You have to understand that you are fearfully and wonderfully made (Psalm 139:14), and the uniqueness and complexity of your individual body speaks volumes to how awesome God is. Down to that part of your body that you think is flawed, He made you that way and you are beautiful.

Some of us, especially us young ladies, can never be completely confident in who we are and what we stand for, if we do not like what we see in the mirror. To the younger me, love your reflection so you can gain the confidence you need to begin living a purposeful life, on purpose. God created you in His image (Genesis 1:27), and He is perfect. So, in His eyes, you are perfect too.

Today in your Journal: *What is unique about you that makes you beautiful?*

Day 9: Be Here, Living in the Present Tense, Right Now.

While writing this book God had me learning so much, and at the same time the enemy was attacking me, trying to tell me that I was not good enough for anyone to learn from because I still don't have it together. However, slowly but surely with the help of my husband we told the enemy to move out of my way. There was one thing that my husband told me that really sat with me. He said that when he was younger his mother would always tell him to not worry about what happened yesterday or focus on those consequences but live better for what is going on right now in the present day. It is very important that you know each day is another opportunity to do better than you did yesterday. You must be present and live in what is going on right now. You should never feel like you do not have the opportunity to change how things are or have been.

In school, I would often try out for sports teams, vocal groups, or solos in band; and, I'd literally beat myself up if I did not get casted for certain parts or placed on a starting team. This had me beating myself up inside just worrying about how I could have done better, replaying my mistakes, and comparing myself to other people. Knowing what I know today, I would have been the total opposite. I am currently living in the present right now and have learned to be anxious about nothing (Matthew 6:31-34). I want to offer you this advice that no one told me: the secret of living a healthy life in both your body and mind is to not mourn over your past, worry about your future, or even anticipate your troubles; but live in the right now and do what you can to conquer the moment in excellence.

Living in the present is so crucial to discovering the purpose that God has for you because He needs a canvas that may not be clean and unmarked. However, all He needs is His view to not be obstructed by what you allow to get in the way. To start this journey, you must learn to forgive past hurts, appreciate the moments that God blesses you with, dream about your future while still working hard. Stop worrying, and don't fall in love with past accomplishments because there is still room to grow.

Today in your Journal: *Do you feel like your life is being held hostage because you can't let go of things of the past? What do you need to let go, and what is your first step?*

Day 10: Fear

What is on the other side of fear? To me I find that fear should be redefined; not something that should be the definition of your life. You must always give it an ending because it's only a story of what you "think" may happen in the future. You should allow fear to be your fuel and not your fortress. Fear makes sure that you are able to remain humble and know that you have not arrived. Fear should not be your enemy, but instead see it as ***false, evidence, appearing real***.

Fear sits on the other side of your destiny more than you can imagine. There are many young people that are afraid of stepping outside the box not knowing that on the other side is a life of excellence and fulfillment. When I decided that I wanted to be a life coach for young girls I had many fears. I thought to myself, what if no one wanted to hear what I had to say? I feared your response before I had even met you or knew that you were reading my book, but God told me to write it to empower you and I had to listen.

The enemy has a clever way of creating division between us, God, and our assignments; so he does it best with the spirit of fear. However, God has not given you the spirit if fear (2 Timothy 1:7) but of Power, Love, and self-control. Fear may seem very real, but the Power that God has given you is something that cannot compare to any amount of strength. You must have high expectations for what you are believing God for and not let fear get in the way of that. Being young and facing everything that the world throws at you, the spirit of fear has its way of creeping in, but you must believe in the power that God has given you to overcome beyond measure. You are alive in Christ! Fear not, beloved, know that you have permission to practice your surprise face! God gave you instructions, so be obedient. You will succeed and reach your destiny as long as you stay locked into His love.

Growing up I was terrified to swim because of the horror stories I heard of other people drowning or a girl's perm reacting with the water & her hair fell out. So, I went nowhere near a chlorine pool until one day my swim teacher pushed me off the diving board into a 12-foot pool. I was only ten years old, under water hearing nothing but my own heart beating and seeing nothing but bubbles as I thought I was taking my last breath. I then kicked my feet, moved my arms, and emerged from the water; and, I saw my classmates there clapping. It was such a joyous moment for me because I did it, and I've loved the water ever since. I am no Olympic star swimmer but if I have to get in the water and doggie paddle with my son; I am no longer afraid. That was such a pivotal moment in my life. From then on, I learned to not let fear define me because, when I emerged from that water, I felt as if I have arrived!

Today in your Journal: *What is on the other side of your fear? What are you expecting God to do in your life?*

Day 11: Mistakes = Excellence

Excellence should be your aim as a kingdom man or woman, but, if you make mistakes, it's okay. We have to first look at the difference between excellence and perfection. Perfection is easily defined as the condition, state, or quality of being free or as free as possible from all flaws or defects. But, we are all so flawed, and in some cases our flaws are what make us unique and loved by many. Excellence (2 Corinthians 8:7), on the other hand, is not associated with perfection at all. It simply means that you do all that you can with what you have at that moment in time.

As a teenager, I often made mistakes and would dwell on them so much because I was so focused on being perfect instead of striving for excellence. My view on excellence then was so distorted because I often compared myself to others. I was always marked as being one of the smartest girls in high school; but, my sophomore year I was met with a humbling (1 Peter 5:6-7) experience when I was failing math tests left and right. Having to ask for help was something that I just wasn't into doing, but I had to. I was so focused on what happened and the mistakes that I couldn't focus on what was going on right now. I realized it was okay to make mistakes as long as you try your best to learn from them and focus on striving for excellence in the future.

Paul teaches us not to dwell on the past and our past mistakes (Philippians 3:12-14). We must always look towards what is in front of us and press forward. Although, you must learn from yesterday you can't continue to live in it and punish yourself for making mistakes. You don't get rid of yesterday by dwelling on it all the time but as you continue to look ahead, the effect it has on your life gets smaller and smaller as you move forward in excellence. As I continued to focus on striving towards excellence, who would have thought that the next year, after tutoring and striving, I'd wind up being placed in advanced math?

Nowadays, it seems like the generations ahead of me have so much more to focus on and even more things to get them distracted. If I could give myself advice back then, I would say, "Jasmine, your success is not based on how many mistakes you did not make, but rather how you pushed past your own expectations and focused on God's. Stop looking in your review mirror as you are driving forward; that is a distraction that can have you crash. Instead of striving for success as the world views it; strive for excellence!

Worldly success is often based on how much money you have or the accolades you receive; but, although that is seen as good, it is only available to a few people. Excellence, however, is available to all! Yes, you will make mistakes (James 3:2), but learn to use them as stepping stones to reach your destiny. Excellence is not based on how you compare to others, but rather how you compare to your own potential of how God sees you. It's okay to not be perfect; do not quit or give up on hope because your life will never be without mistakes. Today, change your mindset; and, instead of asking yourself what if I fail, ask yourself what if you fly?

Today In your Journal: *Write about a time when you made a mistake, how did you handle the situation? Was it only considered a mistake because you were aiming for perfection and not excellence?*

Day 12- Never be Tasteless

Adolescence can be tricky because it's defined as the transitional stage of physical and psychological development that generally occurs during the period from puberty to legal adulthood. And, as we know any transition can be something that, when handled with care, can go great. But, without care, it can be a disaster! When I look back on how my "adolescent years" went, it was the time when I was most vulnerable and susceptible to both good and bad influences. Fortunately, I had turned my focus to more good than bad influences; but, have you heard the phrase "one egg ruins the whole batch?" That became the story of my life. I would see pictures of other girls, whether it be celebrities or girls I went to school with, and I wanted to be them so bad. In a picture of how perfect they appeared to be; and I wanted that so very bad.

I learned the hard way that being who God called me to be is the very best version of myself that I will ever be. I often struggled with wanting to be like everyone else, rather than who I knew God said I was. Mimicking who these women were in magazines or the girls that I saw in school led me on the road of becoming tasteless. Matthew 5:13 explains how we are to be the salt and light of the earth, meaning that we must both help people experience, taste, and see the Kingdom through and around us. My advice to you is not to conform to any external authority because you run the risk of not being authentic or being hypocritical to your true inner self or who God has called you to be. Being a Kingdom man or woman is not easy, but you must learn that your salt & light must be used and exercised so you do not become tasteless.

Do not ever try to hide behind what you "think" you should be; be who you know you are! You are the righteousness of God (Matthew 5:1-6). In no way am I telling you to leave school, get a bible, and go to the bus stop to recite bible verses all day out loud. However, I am telling you to be visible to those who are lost! Do not be afraid to tell others about God and how He is helping to shape your life.

      Rewinding my life I noticed that I was sometimes about acknowledging that I knew who God was. We are commanded to let it happen and not hide our faith (Psalm 34:8), as we are blessed to see how good God is. You may have some unsaved friends or friends who do not attend church, but don't let them influence you. You influence them! Be the salt and do not deny your God (Matthew 10:33) because He is good! Your role in life is to be the salt and light in the world; and, push past the hindrances and compromises that come with settling to be like the world, so you can be comfortable. Having God be pleased with you is a greater feeling than being comfortable. There is much evidence that shows when we depart from the Spirit-led lifestyle and lose our taste; the line between you and the world becomes blurred, and it's hard to get that definition back, much like salt. What good is salt if it has no flavor at all? However, you can secure your light, saltiness, and flavor by remaining focused on Christ and being obedient to Him.

Today in your Journal: *How can you shine your light and be the salt of the Kingdom to your peers? What Godly influences can you have on your peers, or how can you get better?*

Day 13: Your Pace, Your Race

The process to purpose is sure! (Psalm 34:19) Growing up, it seems like everything is timed, as you are always being assessed for this and compared to someone when it comes to test scores or awards for merit. But, God does not work like that. As you are on your journey to discovering your purpose it is very important to remember that this is your race and no one else's. There is no point in time when you should look up and wonder why someone is walking in their purpose and you are not. In Ecclesiastes 3:1 it explains to us that there is a season to everything, and a time to every purpose under the heavens. This means that despite the road and detours that you may face in life; none of them are permanent.

When I was younger it was hard for me to understand that God had a plan and purpose for my life because I was going through so much unnecessary nonsense. Later in life, I found out that everything I went through was very necessary because those seasons and situations helped me develop into the person I am today. Had I not gone through half of the things that God brought me through, I would not have been able to write this book to help guide you through these very sensitive adolescent years. Failing or falling short of the things I knew I needed to do was often a huge hang up for me. I would cry and soak in shame, often wanting to give up; that was all wrong. If you are going through something right now, don't give up (Galatians 6:9)! Trust the process! This is very important because when we are struggling God sees our hard work and, if we do not give up, we will reap a harvest!

I found myself pregnant at 19. After going to college and excelling at everything else, I was now a statistic; another unwed teenage mother from Atlantic City. Devastated, as I beat myself up over this mistake; but with the help of God, I realized I was not alone or a single mother because He is my Father and my child's Father. God had a purpose for my life; and, after going through everything with raising my child, working and still finishing school on time, I realized what that purpose was. In the meantime, of course, I had classmates who became professionals before me, or were able to go to law school and travel the world. However, God put me exactly where He needed me to be.

    As I began my professional career I found myself working with teenage mothers who had the desire to go to college and become hard working citizens, but they had so many people tell them that they couldn't. And, here I was, someone who had made it through, telling them that they could. I often tell my clients to trust the process and finish your race at your own pace because God is going to see you through as long as you let Him in. Younger me, you are like Gold! (Exodus 19:5) You are not going to walk into your purpose shiny and complete. God is going to see you through some things that are going to make you feel like you want to quit, but don't! You have to trust that He is going to see you through every detour in the road, even the ones that you created for yourself! He will help you! Never compare yourself to anyone and always be the best version of yourself that you can be.

Today in Your Journal: *What is one thing that you have gone through that has truly been a process? Knowing what you know now, how could you overcome that season better?*

Day 14: Who are your friends?

In High school, I am pretty sure things go the same way they did when I was younger. You have cliques and lots of them. Back in the day (I always wanted to say that), there was a clique for every interest that you had whether it be the popular girls and makeup or the smart girls and marine biology. I found myself somewhere in between. It took me a while to become part of a group, but when I did I went full out! We dressed alike, acted the same, fought together, and cried together; I thought they would be there until the end. I noticed after some time went by that we really didn't have much in common outside of school unless I pretended to be into what they were into. This group of girls were into some pretty mature things for being freshman in high school and like a follower, I tried to keep up.

Growing up, I knew right from wrong; I went to church, but so did these other girls. I felt like they should've been as convicted as I was, doing things we had no business doing; but they weren't. They would often laugh at me or pressure me into doing things I didn't want to until I would finally give in. One day my friend told me to lie to my mom and tell her I was going to a show at the community center with her and her mother was dropping us off. The very second I began my lie, the conviction crept in. Although, I went through with the lie, when I got off the phone with my mother I told my friend I changed my mind. She clowned me for a half hour because she really wanted to see these boys, and all I kept saying was how wrong it was. Long story short, I went, we saw the boys, and we kissed the boys, and hung out all night on the boardwalk.

When I got home my mother was waiting, one of her friends told her they saw me and described me down to my white leather jacket. I really had my behind handed to me that night. Later that week not only was I punished but I also got very sick, and had a hard time eating; that boy gave me mono! Thankfully, I had a good doctor who got me right together, but I was so embarrassed and my friend that pressured me into going laughed at me for a month. Now, was she really my friend? Friends sharpen one another to do better, not worse (Proverbs 17:17). She was bad company (1 Corinthians 15:33).

It is very important that you learn stay connected God throughout everything that you are going through. And, anyone who tries to deter you from God is only pulling you away from the anointing that He has on your life. God is the true Vine Dresser and you must stay connected (John 15:1-11) not allowing others to disconnect you or distract you. Just as a grape grower who prunes his vines to get rid of the "sucker shoots" that pull away from the nourishment in the grapevines, you must do this also when it comes to your friends.

Today in Your Journal: *Are your friends a help, harm, or hindrance (sucker shoots?) Categorize each friend and write down the reasons why you feel that way.*

Day 15: Healthy Decisions

Life can throw you curveballs that may have you thinking you have to make quick decisions, but you don't. I considered myself to live a very fast life where things that I did would be spontaneous because of the people that I surrounded myself with. Later in my teenage years, I found that all the anxiety and quick decision making would be something that turned my life upside down.

In high school everyone had similar goals; one popular one was to get a job. My senior year of high school I worked at a local coffee shop, but I thought I needed something more to prepare for college. So with that thought in mind, I went on a hunt for a job. I came across an advertisement on the internet that was looking for an administrative assistant. I thought I would be able to do that, besides it was only typing and filing papers. So, I called the number and the guy told me his office was under construction. He said he was holding interviews in a hotel room at one of the casinos in Atlantic City. That sounded so weird to me. So, I asked him if we could meet at the library, to which he responded no because he had plenty interviews, but the job would be mine if I would just come. I was so anxious to work, but something (the Holy Spirit) told me not to go, so I didn't.

Later that week, I found out one girl did go and she was kidnapped and human trafficked out of the state. That could have been me! Philippians 4:6-7 tells us not be anxious in anything, especially decision making. We should always consult with God as a way of securing and dealing our decisions. I understand I was young and so are you, but if you lack the wisdom (James 1:5) to make decisions on your own, God will ultimately see you through; you just have to ask. Learning how to make healthy decisions can really impact how soon you reach your purpose in life. God's timing may be lined up, but one foolish decision (Proverbs 12:15) you make without counsel can send you on an unnecessary detour that could have been avoided.

Today in your Journal: *Have you ever made an unhealthy decision, if you could do it all over again- what would you do differently?*

Day 16: Who inspires you?

 Meeting, reading about, and interacting with people who have inspired me is one of the biggest reasons why I am able to be as effective as I am today. Over the years, I have learned that inspiration isn't just posting a quote on social media and attaching it to a completely non-related picture; but it is truly the process of being mentally stimulated to do or feel something. So, I ask you, who inspires you? Is there someone in your life or someone that you follow online and read about that truly "gets it"? They speak to your soul and put you in the place to follow through with acting out your destiny?

 Over the years, I have learned that you are equal to the average of the top five people you associate with, or whose material you digest through hearing or reading. As a young person my inspiration would be placed upon many negative people that would often steer me in the wrong direction. Sometimes, as kids we may not have people right in front of us that are able to inspire us, so we then must seek God (1 John 4:1) to give us where to find that inspiration. I grew up in a neighborhood in Atlantic City where there weren't many role models around, other than those in my own family, but I sought greater. I found my inspiration in books, positive TV sitcoms, and videos that I would see of women who looked like me making changes in their communities. I knew from a very young age that I was destined for greater; I just needed a push.

 If you feel like someone around you is truly inspiring, you to be better and they are reachable; talk to them. There is nothing wrong with letting someone know that they inspire you; maybe if you let them know they can give you insight on something that you don't already know. In Matthew 7:7, it says ask and things will be given unto you, so how do you know what that person may say if you do not seek them?

Today in your Journal: *Who inspires you and why?*

Day 17: Broken Crayons still color & Dirty Hands still Pray

We have all been broken! However, the truth is that we must all understand that God is able to see us through the brokenness. Just like a box of broken, paperless, worn down crayons; He can see through the small and shattered pieces, and is able to use them to create something uniquely beautiful. He is the master creator! (Isaiah 61:1-7)

Growing up, I did not know this. I have been broken at times to the point where I would not care about anything or anyone, even myself. The brokenness that I experienced came from disappointments, regret, heartaches, and not understanding my worth; just to name a few. As a teenager, one of the lowest points in my life was when I found myself in situations that could have easily been avoided had I not thought my brokenness was the end.

At the age of 13, I found myself contemplating suicide because I was no longer a virgin. I was in a bad place because I knew that what I did was wrong. I also knew that I was forced into making a decision that could have changed my whole life, if something had gone wrong. I felt as if my innocence was taken away from me, and I knew that it was something that I would never get back. That boy broke my heart and took it with him, and I felt as if I had nothing left.

Every night following that "2-minute thrill", I would think about what could have gone wrong. What if I had gotten pregnant, contracted a disease, or what if someone found out? My parents would kill me, and I knew that the kids at school would whisper about me and call me names. There were often days that I would look myself the mirror and ask myself, "Why are you still here?" I wanted to die because I was no longer untouched, new, and perfect like a brand-new box of crayons. Fortunately, after a night of counseling with my Spiritual Mother, I did not commit suicide. And, I am here today to help you get through your period of brokenness.

Psalm 34:18 states that The LORD is near to the brokenhearted and saves those who are crushed in spirit. When your spirit is crushed, you have regrets, and you feel like your mistakes are too much to go back from; remember that your biggest "failures" or "mistakes" in your eyes is what God uses the most. The enemy has a way of tricking us to believe that we are worthless because we are worn down, broken, and afraid of pushing through what life is giving us. Your regret may run deep from the things that you have done; however, today younger me, do not throw away or waste your broken crayons. They still color!

I know that sometimes you feel broken, ugly, and useless, however God is there to heal everything that we are going through and create a masterpiece. During those times that you feel broken, be it from a choice you made or life just happening; remember that, despite all you have gone through, (no matter how dirty, broken, and useless you feel) you can still pray that God restore you through your brokenness and pick up all the pieces that were once scattered (Deuteronomy 30:3-13).

Today in your Journal: *Are you living with shame or regret from your past? Do you feel like it's preventing God from using you the way that he needs to? If so, forgive that person, situation, or yourself. How will you do that?*

Day 18: Stop Making Excuses

Excuses are something that we all make when we are either too lazy or genuinely feel inadequate of taking on or completing a task. Throughout my life I have found myself not wanting to do something unless I knew beyond a shadow of doubt that I can complete it with little or no effort. This was a huge issue of mine. I would procrastinate or not challenge myself because I was afraid of failure; and ultimately, I was getting away from what I knew God was telling me to do all along. For example, during the process of writing this book I would often tell myself I didn't have the time or expertise, and God knew differently. Just like Moses (Exodus 3:11-15), I had so many excuses growing up.

The fact of the matter is, God will always be with you and see you through things that He has ordained. No matter how often we have the "Who? Me?" complex. If your spirit is telling you that there is something God wants you to do, do it afraid, but do it. There are many things that I look back on which I knew I should have done, I but didn't. I let fear get in the way, and I made excuses. If God can take a stuttering murderer (Exodus 4:10) with no experience in what He was asking him to do, and have him perform glorious works; what is stopping you?

Today in your Journal: *What excuses are you making to not do what God has called you to do? When are you going to stop making excuses and get to work?*

Day 19: Your Haters are required to witness your Glow Up

Compliments, awards, and recognition was something that I never took well. I was shy, very shy. I hated to be the center of attention because the kids that I grew up with made it seem like doing good was bad. That was so backwards. I never truly understood why God would place me in the light to be seen by others when I had accomplished something. But, when I got older I understood my influence was necessary not just for them, but me as well.

Psalm 23:5 says "You prepare a table before me in the presence of my enemies. You anoint my head with oil; my cup overflows." Mrs. J told me, when I was 12, that I was anointed; and, if I did what God asked of me, my blessings would overflow. Overflow they did! Obedience can lead you to see overflow in a way that you would never imagine.

My enemies were different; they hated me for doing well and being happy. Do you have people like that in your life? If so, get away from them now! Don't allow their presence to influence you so much that you begin to think that your well-doing is bad. Your accomplishments are a direct result of your hard work! You are going to accomplish many great things in your life. Just don't be like me and hide your good works from your haters because you are afraid of not being "cool" in their eyes. In no way am I saying to mingle with them and allow them to further step on your name (Matthew 7:6) but, be the positive peer that they need to see. You are more of an influence than you believe yourself to be.

Today in your Journal: *Do you have haters or bullies in your life? If so what do they hate you for? Do you feel as though it's a valid reason? Why or why not?*

Day 20: SMART Goals

In school, you would always hear your teacher say that it is important to set as many goals as you can; but have they ever taught you how to properly set a goal? In high school, I had one English teacher that would always have us write down these unattainable goals; and throw a whole fit when we didn't reach them. I would often set goals for myself that did not make any sense or seem realistic because I was still comparing myself to others in the process. It is great to have goals, but you should always set SMART goals for yourself that are specific, measurable, achievable, relevant, and time bound. This allows what you do and what you plan, with God's direction to be strategically placed to where you may see them come to fruition one day.

During your journey towards understanding your purpose and who you are spiritually, you will embark on many assignments. These assignments will sometimes alter your life so much that they will require planning and goal-setting on your part. You must make sure that, when you are given these assignments, you hear from God loud and clear as to what he wants you to do, because if you have Him through the process you will never fail.

I wish someone would have told me to be diligent (Proverbs 21:5) when it came to my goals and the assignments that God have given me because it would have saved me much trouble. When you are given assignments and setting goals, be courageous (2 Chronicles 15:7) with your planning; and stay strong throughout the process because it will all be so worth it!

Today in your Journal: *What is one goal that you have now? Write down that goal and identify the reasons that make it a SMART goal: Specific, Measurable, Achievable, Relevant, & Time Bound*

Day 21: Lean on Me- The Importance of Mentorship

I never knew how important it was to have a mentor until I was almost in my mid 20's; however, I wish I had known sooner. It is so vitally important to have someone there who can guide you through this thing called "life." Mentoring has two definitions both biblically and secularly. The dictionary defines mentorship as the teaching or giving advice or guidance to someone, such as a less experienced person or child. Biblically, it is explained that Jesus mentored His disciples during His ministry on earth. In fact, He said anyone who serves Him must follow Him (John 12:26). So, to simplify that is Jesus your mentor? Or, do you have a mentor that believes in Jesus, as you do, that can guide you along the right path? Someone who can help you and warn you of the things ahead that you may not be able to see?

I know most of you may remember the saying WWJD? (What would Jesus do?) This reminded people of doing as Jesus would when life throws you different situations. I learned over the years to take the lemons life threw me and make the best lemonade that I could. It's amazing how you can turn something sour and tart into something sweet and refreshing when you have God leading you. It is also a beautiful thing when you have someone who has an intimate relationship with God leading you through all that life may bring you. As we embark on the ending of the life lessons I've given you, I'm sure there are some lessons you still have questions about that were not mentioned; but you don't have to search far for those answers. Pray and ask God to bring someone into your life that can be your mentor. Or, if you need some guidance connect yourself with a mentorship program that can help you find the perfect mentor for you specifically.

Today in your Journal: *Do you have a mentor? If so, what makes them a good mentor for you? If not, list the qualities you would like your mentor to have.*

Note from the Author:

You are well on your way to living a purposeful life. I pray that you understand more about yourself and your purpose now than when you first started this journey. As a wise man once said, "The only impossible journey is the one that you never began." You have arrived beloved! I commend you for taking the time to invest in yourself and be obedient to what God has assigned & called you to do.

With Love,

Your Purpose Partner, Jasmine J. Moore

P.S- For Daily inspiration, motivation, and future events follow me on Facebook @Jasmine J. Moore -Purpose Partner***

Made in the USA
Middletown, DE
24 June 2024